HOT AND COLD AND IN BETWEEN

by ROBERT FROMAN

Illustrated by RICHARD CUFFARI

Published by GROSSET & DUNLAP, INC., New York

HOT AND COLD
AND IN BETWEEN

Fire feels hot.

Ice feels cold.

The bricks of a fireplace feel warm when a fire is burning.

The side of a refrigerator feels cool.
Why do these things feel the way they do?

You can make a test to help you find out why.

Ask your mother for three bowls or pots to put water in.

From the hot water tap put enough water in the first bowl to fill it about halfway.

Make sure the water is hot but not too hot to hold your hand in.

From the cold water tap put enough water in the second bowl to fill it about halfway, too.

Make sure the water is quite cold.

Put a mixture of hot water and cold water in the third bowl so that it, too, is about half full.

Try to mix this water so that it feels neither warm nor cool to your hands.

It will be all right if it is just a little warm or just a little cool.

Line up the three bowls of water in the sink or on the drainboard.

Put the one with hot water on the left.

Put the one with cold water on the right.

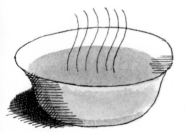 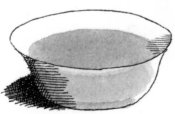 

Put the third bowl in the middle.

Put your left hand in the bowl of hot water, and put your right hand in the bowl of cold water.

Leave them there for about a minute.

At the end of the minute take your hands out of the bowls on the right and left and put both hands in the bowl in the middle.

Are you surprised?

Now the water in the middle bowl feels different than before.

It also feels different to your left hand from the way it feels to your right hand.

It feels cold to your left hand.

It feels hot to your right hand.

Can you guess why the water in the middle bowl feels different to each hand?

The reason is very important and very interesting.

The reason is that when something feels hot or warm or cool or cold, what you feel is the *flow* of HEAT.

And HEAT always flows from something warmer to something cooler.

Fire is warmer than your hands, so HEAT flows from
the fire to your hands.

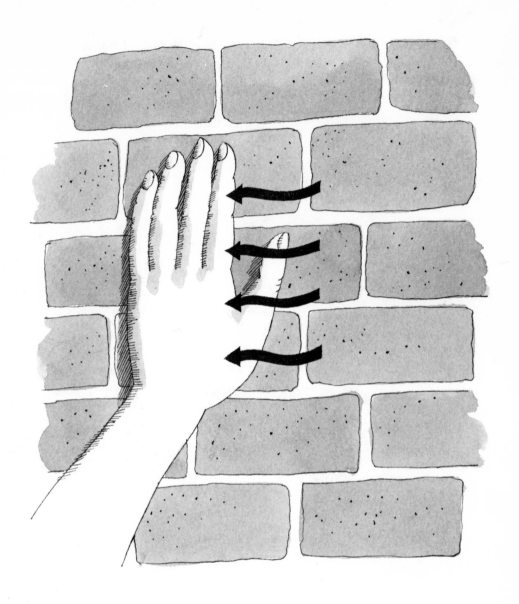

The fireplace bricks are warmer than your hands, too.
HEAT flows from the bricks into your hands.

But what happens when you hold an ice cube in your hand?

Is there something called COLD which flows the way
HEAT flows?

No.

This is wrong.

There is *no* something called COLD which flows the
way HEAT flows.

What you feel when you hold an ice cube in your
hand is the flow of HEAT just as when you hold your
hands out to a fire.

But this time the flow goes the other way.

Your hand is warmer than an ice cube.

So when you hold an ice cube, HEAT flows from your hand to the ice.

Cold is not something you *gain* from the ice cube.

Cold is the way you feel because you *lose* HEAT to the ice cube.

You feel hot when you gain HEAT.

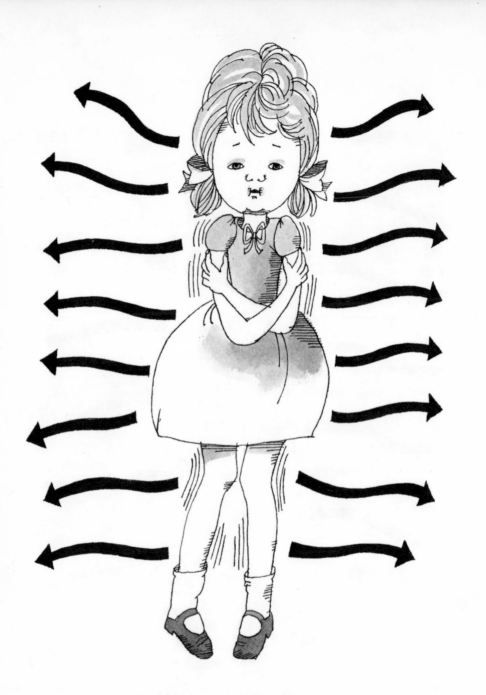

You feel cold when you lose HEAT.

Your hand is warmer than the side of a refrigerator.

When you hold your hand against the side of the refrigerator, HEAT flows from your hand to the refrigerator.

Now do you know what happened when you held your left hand in hot water and your right hand in cold water for a minute,
then moved your hand to the middle bowl?

What happened was that when you held your left hand in hot water the water sent HEAT into that hand.

This made your left hand hotter, because when anything gains HEAT it grows hotter.

The cold water took HEAT from your right hand.

This made your right hand colder, because when anything loses HEAT it grows colder.

Then you put both hands in the middle bowl.
Now HEAT flowed from your hot left hand into the
water of the middle bowl.

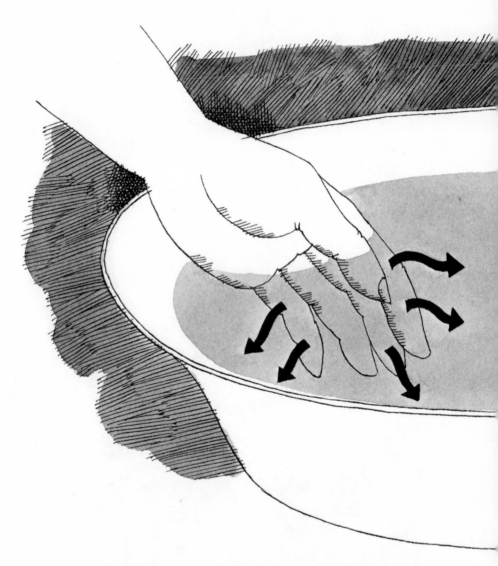

This made the water feel cold to your left hand.

At the same time HEAT flowed from the water of
the middle bowl into your cold right hand.

This made the water feel hot to your right hand.

Can you guess what would happen if you went out in bright sunshine on a hot summer day?

You would feel hot, very hot.

HEAT would flow all over you from the sun.

34

HEAT also would flow to you from the pavement you stand on and from the brick walls around you.

You can escape from some of this flow of HEAT.

If you step into the shade of a tree, the tree blocks the flow of HEAT from the sun.

If you go into a house, its walls block the flow of HEAT from the pavement and from the brick walls of the buildings.

Can you guess what would happen if you went out
in a swimsuit on a snowy winter day?

You would feel cold, very cold.

HEAT would flow from all parts of you into the air and the ground.

You can stop some of that HEAT flow with clothes.

With many heavy clothes you can stop most of the
HEAT flow.

Can you find something that feels neither hot nor warm nor cool nor cold?

Try the cover of this book.

Try the top of the nearest table or desk.

Try feeling your forehead with your hand.

Try feeling the fingertips of your left hand with the fingertips of your right hand.

It is not easy to find something that feels neither hot nor warm nor cool nor cold.

HEAT is restless.

It moves from something warmer to something cooler whenever it gets the chance to do so.

When your fingers are even just a little cooler than something they touch, HEAT flows to them and the thing touched feels warm.

When your fingers are even just a little warmer than something they touch, HEAT flows from them and the thing touched feels cool.

That is why almost all the things you touch—even different parts of your own body—feel at least a little warm or a little cool.

Whenever two things meet, there almost always is at least a little flow of HEAT between them.